World Peace: The Voice of a Mountain Bird

World Peace: The Voice of a Mountain Bird

Amit Ray and Banani Ray

Inner Light Publishers
www.inner-light-in.com

PART ONE

I was flying over the mountain. It was a wonderful morning. I was singing in joy. Suddenly, I noticed them. I was scared. Who are those strange looking people? They looked alien to our peaceful mountain terrain. What the hell are they doing here? They are carrying large barrels in their hands. I got suspicious. I hovered over them a few times, trying to inspect them closely. I sensed impending death and calamity looming over the valley and the mountain. I didn't know how this bad omen came to my mind. But it made me shaky.

I am a tiny mountain bird. I live on the top of a Pine tree at the foot of the mountain. Humans rarely visit this terrain except a few villagers from the other side of the mountain. We seldom find strangers here. These people are looking harmless till now. But I couldn't ignore the foreboding of my mind. I must do something. At all cost I'll try to protect our lovely land. I flew to my nest, a little restless and anxious.

I have a lovely family down there in my nest. We — me and my mate Chico built the cozy nest for me to lay eggs and raise my kids. I have two adorable kids— a little boy and a little girl. They are still very young. They hobble on their tiny legs— still didn't learn to fly. Their eyes have just opened and tiny feathers started to grow on their tender skin. It will take them a few days to be able to fly up to low branches. Then we'll teach them how to find food and what to eat. We are excited to see them growing day by day.

My wonderful partner Chico guards them while I'm out to gather food for the kids. Of course, most of the time, he gathers the food while I guard the children. Our little family is very happy in our cute little nest. We have hardly any interest in things outside our little world.

My tree stands on the bank of a mountain stream, which flows like a serpent along the valley. I love seeing the beautiful river dancing downwards. She is mysterious and gorgeous during the monsoon, and colorful during the autumn when she holds in her bosom the reflection of the colorful forest around. Her silvery shallow stream twines gracefully through the towering mountains, running out slowly, coiling itself occasionally to rest in deep, quiet pools.

Our mountain is wild, beautiful, and rich in colors. It is heavily forested, covered by trees and shrubs. Trees are the greatest charms of this mountain. The delightful Pine trees, the magnificent Oaks, the graceful Deodars and the endless Willows, Birch and Poplars adorn the mountain in red and green and gold.

In the springtime the fresh green tints on the trees and mountain are refreshing to the eye. In the autumn the trees change colors from green to silvery grey to delicate russet, with a red tone on the stems and branches. Some of them turn crimson red in color and some stand tall like the golden poles in to the sky.

Part of the mountain is forbidding and surrounded by nearly impenetrable wilderness. It is a world of twilight and darkness, among dense stands of tall, virgin forests, where the interplay of light and shadows are woven like a sweet soundless melody. It is a beautiful, peaceful and unspoiled terrain on earth.

Trees are wonderful beings. What a bountiful and gracious life they live – giving, giving and giving. They are epitome of silent, unassuming charity. They give us the fresh air, shades, shelters, fruits, flowers, and even woods, when they die. Most humans do not understand the value of their mute service. They take them for granted. What a pity! I have made friends with the trees on the mountain. Almost every tree on the mountain knows me. I sit on them, dance on them and send them my good wishes.

Every day I send silent gratitude to the Pine tree that holds us and our nest. She understands our emotion and responds to our loving embrace. I sense the joy of my tree when I sing and dance on her branches.

I feel that trees are brave souls enriching lives and adorning mother earth with their nourishing presence. I love them. I love everything in my tiny world. I love the nourishing Earth that produces seeds and grains in plenty. I love the river and her refreshing clear water. I love the clean mountain air. I love the clear blue sky and I love the Sun, the golden disk that keeps us warm. I am so happy, and grateful and contented to be here on mother earth.

On the farthest side of the mountain there is a spring that is cold during the summer and warm in the winter. The mountain people regard this lake with great sanctity.

There is a small village on the other side of my mountain. Simple mountain folks live there. The valley between the ranges is lush green, carpeted with grass and fringed with the Daisies, where the villagers bring their cattle to graze upon. During

13

the monsoon, they grow grains in the valley. Monsoon is a great feasting time for us.

How I admire this magical, mystical place on earth where peace reigns supreme. The shady trees and the songs of the bees lull us into serene fantasy and daydream.

When the Sun shines bright in the morning I love to sing sitting on the summit of my tree – it is my drawing room. I sing to my heart's content in the sheer joy of singing. I love to sing the song of my soul. I have a wonderful resonant voice. I take delight in my voice. I know somewhere someone is listening.

I dance and play with the wind. Down the tree, just above the river a branch bends down towards the river, almost touching it. I love to sit on the edge of the branch and sway in the wind. It's my play room. Often times, I would swoop down to the ground at the base of my beloved Pine tree. This is one of my favorite games.

I am a happy bird. I am happy with my little life, in my little nest. My flight and my wings are my liberation from the daily trivialities. I fly far and near and I see the world from above. I feel a strange freedom when I am on my wings. The clear sky is my inspiration to fly. It gives me the taste of freedom. I love to soar in the boundless sky. In the vast emptiness of the blue, my soul rejoices listening to the soundless music of the wind. I never feel the weight of my wings. The empty air always takes care of me.

I don't know exactly how I learnt flying. I believe that the grand teacher introduced it into my genes. When I was little, no one taught me how to fly. I was scared to jump out of my nest.

"A bird is safe in its nest - but that is not what its wings are made for," my dad used to say. One day he pushed me into the empty sky. I was falling below towards the ground. My eyes were turned upwards into the empty sky. Suddenly the air takes care of me like a caring mother. Like an angel I learned to synchronize my wings with the air.

I love the freedom of my wings. I love the empty space above the ground. I rejoice in my freedom. Freedom is my religion. Peace is my God. Love is my worship. I am completely happy with my little life, in my small world. I live in contentment with a thankful heart. I love my family. I love my neighbors. I love all living beings. I love the freedom of my mind.

I have friendly neighbors. My immediate neighbor is a family of Yellow-billed blue Magpie. They are very handsome with their blue and white plumage and long tail feathers. They are quite a noisy bunch. They often keep up with their incessant chattering in their loud ringing voice.

On the Oak tree next to them lives my friend the Grey-winged Blackbird. What a rich and full voice he has! His melodious song echoing in the valley makes me so peaceful and contemplative.

Just opposite to my Pine tree there is a big flock of red billed Choughs on the tree. They have black plumage and bright red feet. I love to hear their resonant call. On the tall Birch tree, there is a family of Redbreast Robins. They too, like us, have very young kids in their nest.

Far across the river, on an old Juniper tree resides a flock of Short-billed Minivets. When the flock flies from one tree to another making pleasant low-note twittering, they make a gorgeous view, as the bright scarlet and black of the males and the yellow and grey of the females dazzle in the sunlight.

We also have the Starlings, Greenfinches, Red brow Goldfinches and Brown and Grey Wagtails in our forest colony.

There is another neighbor worth mentioning. They are a pair of song-thrush— the grey headed Ouzels, with their ashy white crown, yellow feet and blackish tail. I often find the mister sitting on the summit of their tall fir tree and singing at the approach of the evening. Their notes are so charming. His spouse has laid five eggs this summer — bluish white egg, thickly mottled with brown tints. I often visit their tree. I love to listen to their song.

Our world is peaceful, whole and complete. It is almost perfect. We love each other. We rejoice in the company of one another, and there is a strange bond of fraternity among us.

PART TWO

The golden rays of the morning Sun have just peeped through the leaves. I woke up early in the dawn, long before the glint of the sun found its way through the forests of Pine. I flew atop the tree to sit in my drawing room and sing. The fresh mountain breeze caresses my feathers, and my heart breathes in peace. My song serves as a wake-up call for Chico, who, you know, is a little lazy. He flies to sit beside me, and together we sing to welcome the new day.

After a while, it becomes a little noisy as the air becomes musical with the twittering of our feathered colony. The Blue-Magpies, our noisy neighbors, begin their chattering as the Sun rises over the mountain top. I flew back to my nest to wake up my fledglings.

The air is so pleasant, our nest so cozy, and my children are so cute. I want them to provide a plentiful diet of nice worms and bugs, so they grow up healthy, strong and beautiful. I'm so proud of my babies.

Now it's time to go out to look for food. I darted down to the field, and spotted some tiny seeds on the ground. I was tempted to taste one myself. But on a second thought, I discarded the idea. The kids are hungry. They are waiting for my return. I managed to scoop two seeds on my tiny beak, and flew back to my nest. I thrust the food in to the open beaks of my kids, one by one. As soon as I flew back to my nest, Chico darted away towards the valley. Now it's my turn to guard the kids.

He flew back in a while with some tiny bugs in his beak, and thrust them in the gaping mouth of the kids. It was just then, when I noticed them — my two little human friends. Emma and Asher were standing beneath my Pine tree. These two young siblings come from the village on the other side of the mountain. Their village is beautiful, shaded by tall Pines and Junipers. In their village, they have orchards of apples and apricots, which are watered by a narrow mountain stream. The grassy banks of the stream are streaked with the coral red of the Willow rootlets. Their village has meadows covered by the tender green young rice plants and golden wheat grasses.

I often take delight in visiting their beautiful village. Out through the luxuriant foliage peeps the peasant's cottage, with its tumble-down, thatched gable roof. The village chief and a few affluent families have straw-house granaries — a place frequently visited by our neighbor Starlings, because this is where the villagers store their grains.

My friends come from a poor peasant family. Their dad works on the field of others. Though poor they are, they have ample food, sufficient clothing, a comfortable house and abundant fuel to keep them warm in the winter seasons. Life is terribly earnest for these mountain folks, bereft of any amusement, and the child that can walk can work. There is general comfort, but no luxury. Whenever I visit them in the village, I find their dad working in the field, their mom busy with the household chores. I find her busy pounding rice, wheat or maize in her courtyard or sometimes spinning cotton in her spinning wheel, while her dog Ruba sleeps or rolls in the Sun. Ruba is a lazy dog.

Emma and Asher are often out to look after their cattle. They often make their trail to the river on our side of the mountain through narrow, shadowy footways, established over the eons by the mountain people. The trail runs haphazardly through the virgin forests.

I squeaked in delight to see my young friends. I was so happy to see them. So affectionate towards each other, so gentle and so bright and lively, they seem to bring a streak of sunshine with them whenever they come. They come here almost every alternate day to fetch sweet drinking water from the river and often they take their bath here. They chitchat and play beneath my Pine tree. Emma is older of the two. Asher is still very young.

I love humans. I love these children. Oftentimes they bring food for us. The pieces of bread and biscuits they bring are much more delicious than the grains we find in the field.

I flew down to a lower branch so they could notice me. They were delighted to find me.

"Good morning! How are you, friends?" I chirped in delight. Emma was holding something in her little hands. She threw them on the ground a little away.

"Breads!" I squeaked in joy, "Thank you, Honey!"

I flew down to collect some, and flew back to my nest. My young ones started making delightful noises as I pushed the food in their gaping mouths. Then I flew back to my friends again. I nibbled a few pieces myself, and flew back to my nest carrying a large piece for Chico. He was delighted too. He flew down to collect some more for himself.

Little Asher was clapping his hands seeing us darting to and fro. We had a sumptuous breakfast this morning, thanks to my friends.

I stretched my wings and swooped down to the river to drink its fresh clean water. Emma and Asher were playing in the knee-deep water. They were laughing, teasing each other, and throwing water.

"Be careful, guys," I warned them. "Don't go far."

Emma smiled at me. Such a beautiful and innocent smile she has.

I don't know if they understand my words, but there is a strange communication between us. I understand the feelings and emotion underlying their words, and I think they can understand me too.

My mom and dad lived on a tree close to a tribal dwelling. Dad brought me up after my mom and other siblings passed away in a terrible thunderstorm, when I was only 3 months old.

Dad was my friend, mom and mentor— all in one. He was an extraordinary bird. He was compassionate, caring and wise. I was awed by his wisdom. My dad mastered the art of understanding the feelings and intent of the humans. Just by looking at them he could tell if a person approaching us was harmless or not. He could tell beforehand what a human was thinking even before he uttered any word.

I was awestruck to see that. "How do you understand their words, Dad?" I often asked him.

"Words carry a meaning, my little darling," he used to say. "But if you want to understand the meaning — the feeling and intent, don't concentrate on the words. Concentrate on the sound instead."

"Concentrate on the sound of the words they utter?" I was excited to learn a new thing.

"Right, dear," Dad said. "Sounds are subtler than words, and behind every sound uttered by a human, there is a feelings and intent. Concentrate on the source of the sound, and you'll know their thoughts and feelings even without understanding their language."

This concept was absolutely strange, and unknown to any bird I knew. I was fascinated by this idea. Mastering all my will and concentration, I started working on it. But initially, I failed over and over again. I was disappointed. "This is not for me, Dad," I used to say in frustration. "You are specially gifted with this power."

"No, my child, I'm not," he assured me. "Only I am adept in making my mind silent and quiet. Make your mind quiet and tranquil and you can get under the meanings of the words. Words are just layers masking the feelings." My dad insisted.

"How do I make my mind quiet and tranquil, Dad?"

"Just practice sitting silently, doing nothing, Honey," he instructed me, "and let go of any and all thoughts."

At the encouragement of my dad I kept trying. Every day, in the afternoon, after I had my last food and drink, I quietly sat on the higher branch of a tall Oak tree, facing the setting Sun. I used to sit very silently, while other birdies were chirping and hopping around. Day after day I kept practicing this. I didn't actually expect to attain anything. I did this, just because my dad asked me to do so. Over time this practice just became a pleasant natural ritual, which I looked forward to, throughout the day.

One day suddenly the miracle happened. As I was sitting there in the evening, two boys came there to sit beneath the tree. They were talking about something. Suddenly it occurred to me that I should try to concentrate on the sound of what they are saying. Just as I did so, a veil tore open, and I clearly understood that one boy was telling the other that he didn't have anything to eat the whole day. His dad was seriously ill, and his mom went to the doctor asking for his help.

I was startled to know this. I was happy at my achievement, but sad too, to know their distress. But there was nothing I could do about it.

I flew to my dad to report this. My dad was evidently very happy that he could teach me the skill. However, he looked sad too. "These mountain folks are good people, kind people, my child," he said and sighed. "It would be such a pleasure if we, birds, could help them!" From that day on I could exercise my skill at will. This skill has saved me from bird-catchers and humans with evil intentions, and I have made friends with these two children – Emma and Asher.

PART THREE

I have another human friend in the village— the good old Yashir. He has long hairs and a long flowing beard that are white as the mountain snow. He has bright sparkling eyes and a tall upright gesture. He lives alone in a cottage beneath a regal Oak tree at the border of the village, near a sparkling mountain stream. He has a small apple orchard and a vegetable garden surrounding his cottage.

He understands the languages of birds and animals. He is so loving, serene, and peaceful. I love this wise old man. He loves me too. He lovingly calls me 'Coco.' He brings me a cake, a chocolate dessert or a piece of bread, and soothes me with his loving words, when I am tired or had a rough day. He is so sweet.

In the springtime Yashir keeps ripe apples for me, and oftentimes he makes apple pies. Mmmm! Even now my mouth waters remembering those yummy delicious apple pies! He also makes wonderful pancakes, and feeds me some, whenever I visit him. He is very hospitable.

I feel like flying to him every now and then. He teaches me lessons on life, and I help him keeping his orchard free from bugs and insects.

I visit him almost every day. When I fly across the mountain in the afternoon, I find him sitting on the veranda of his cottage, or sometimes, working in his orchard. We chitchat about this and that, each in our own language. But we completely understand each other. There is absolutely no gap in our communication.

From him I learned lots of things along the way. I have learnt that my life, however insignificant it is, is a gift of the Divine, and I have a unique life purpose. Since knowing this, I live my life in joy and dignity.

Once he said, "My friend, if you want to live a meaningful life, live your life intensely using the wings of compassion and alertness. Live every moment as a sacred celebration."

"But, Yashir," I interrupted him, "life is not all celebration and joy, you know. We have our share of problems too."

"True, my little darling," he said. "Life is not always perfect. Like a road, it has many bends, ups and downs, but that's its beauty."

"But Yashir, we are afraid of tough times," I said in protest.

"Ture!" he agreed. "But, you only get the chance to live this life once. Happiness, or suffering, it will pass away. It always passes away. But always let your light shine bright. Only then you'll triumph over life."

"How do I let my light shine, Yashir?"

Yashir laughed aloud at my persistent questioning.

"Dance to your heart's content, tear open your heart in love, sing the song of your soul, and shine the light of compassion on whoever might need it," he said. "That's the way of light, Coco."

I was awed. "That's brilliant, Yashir," was all I could say.

"You are here to evolve and make your consciousness high," Yashir said again. "You are here to dance, sing and celebrate life. You are here to help others to make their life happy. "

"Don't you sometimes feel discouraged, Yashir?" I asked timidly.

Yashir smiled and caressed my feathers. He looked so handsome even in his old age. "Everything in my life is not perfect, Coco," he said. "There were many new turns, new chapters, which were challenging, to say the least. Many things try to break me down. But I know I have to stand up, and I have to walk forward."

I thanked my old friend for his amazing philosophy of life, and I silently made a commitment to follow his wise advice.

I am open to new ideas. I'm always learning and evolving. I have a tremendous hunger for learning, and I'm learning very fast. I learnt from many of my mistakes and I learnt to forgive myself for my mistakes. I know my limitations but with all my limitations I love myself. Yashir taught me that I have the freedom to be myself.

From him I learnt the value of peace, empathy, kindness, forgiveness and trusting my intuition. Without these, the soul is empty. Yashir says. When our soul is full with empathy and kindness, the feelings of insecurity and fear evaporate.

When my kids will grow up and fly, I'll teach them these invaluable life lessons that I learnt over time from my dad, from my friend Yashir, and from the Life itself.

ℭ ℬ

It was a sultry afternoon. These days are very warm because of the dry seasons. We often rest at home, or go to the shady fields to find those tasty little insects for meal. As I flew back to my nest, Chico flew down to take his bath in the river. After feeding my fledglings, I flew away to an Oak tree at the base of the mountain to pluck some leaves for repairing my nest.

It was then that I noticed those strange fellows at the feet of the mountain. Instinctively I flew away swiftly to a higher branch. Being caught is no fun.

Then I flew higher in the sky and hovered over them a little to keep a close watch on them. These people are not the village tribes I know. They were dressed in uniforms. They were working at a frantic pace. They were building up a place to stay amid the rugged mountain frontier. I narrowed my eyes. What on earth are they doing here?

An ominous foreboding of calamity clouded my mind. I was sensing danger. But then, I brushed my fear aside. True, this was not a usual scene on the mountain, but they are looking harmless till now.

It was being dark. I couldn't wait anymore. I hurriedly flew back to my nest, my home sweet home. Chico and I chitchatted a little before we took off to our dream land, after a long tiring day, enfolding our babes with our warm, soft wings.

PART FOUR

Today I was awake early in the morning. I flew to my favorite place at the top of my tree. I didn't feel like singing. I was sitting silently. The sky was heavy and I sensed an uncanny sensation.

After a while Chico came to sit beside me. He was unusually silent too. What was going on? Did he notice those peculiar people too? As the Sun peeped over the mountain, I flew back to our nest and Chico flew away in search of food.

After a little while he came back with food to feed the children. Again he flew away and brought back two morsels for both of us. I was feeling thirsty. So I flew down to the river to quench my thirst. On my way I noticed Tito, the woodpecker busy tap-tapping on the trunk of a Birch tree. He was catching the bugs in the tree bark with his sharp bill. His merry red cap and broad grey shoulder cape made him very pretty to look at. I was amused seeing him working away in cheerful perseverance.

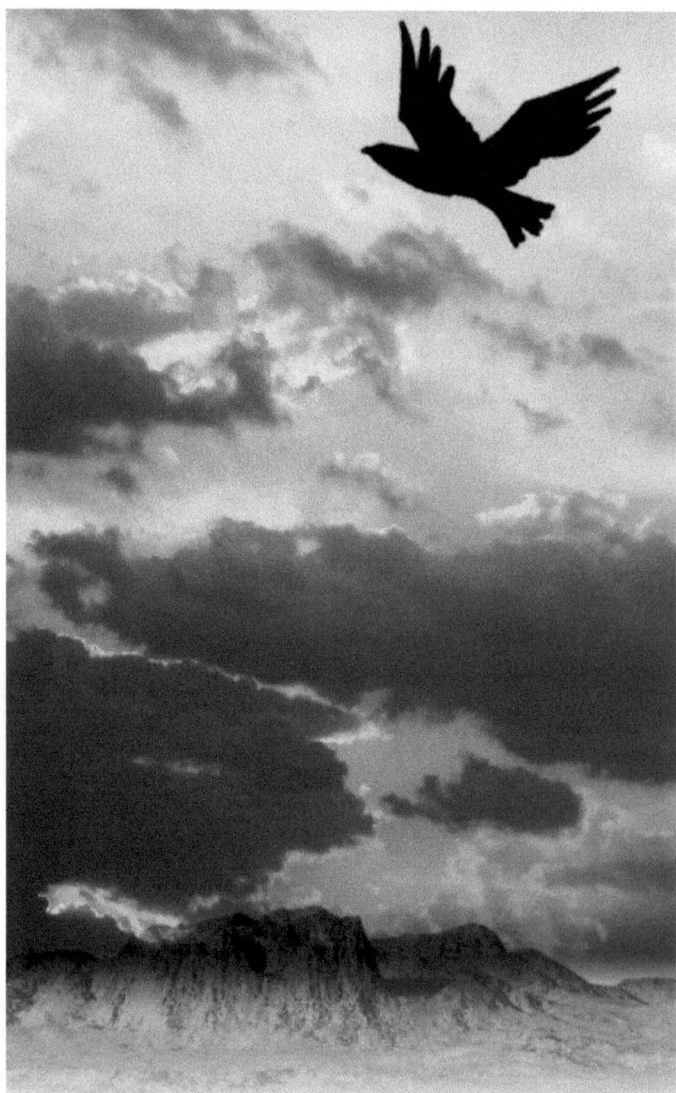

After drinking water, I decided to take a flight in the sky. I soared high and instantaneously my mind became peaceful and happy. Sun was shining bright over head, and I was really enjoying my flight. Suddenly I noticed a peck of dark cloud on the horizon. It made me apprehensive. But my doubt was correct. Soon the cloud started growing in volume until it covered the sky. It scared me out of my skin. Quickly I flew back to my nest, and covered my babies with my wings. I am scared of storm, because it robbed me off my mom and brothers.

Except for the bad thunderstorms, the summers and monsoons are good here, because there are plenty to eat in the forest. But, we, birds, really hate the thunderstorms. Last year, we lost three of our neighbors in the storm. Winters are dreadful too. Food becomes scarce and the cold nights are long and scaring. I love the springtime, when the weather remains clear and sunny. Our little hearts sing in joy as the miseries of cold and the dreary monotony of the winter snow pass away and mother earth comes to life again with all her bright colors of fragrant flowers. Our hearts dance in grateful thanksgiving, as the climate becomes warm and sunny again in the springtime.

But now my mind was wary sensing the imminent danger. I anxiously looked up at the sky. The blue sky was covered by the wings of a monstrous cloud. Dark, ominous clouds were rolling over us, blotting out the sun.

Chico was gravely sitting beside me. We were all alert and apprehensive, ready to take on the impending danger.

The temperature dropped dramatically as Mother Nature set the stage for a really big display of her dreadful power. A light shower arrived first, just enough to dampen us down. But then the main storm struck with all its fury and rage. The force of the wind rocked the tree and a curtain of darkness dropped over us.

Flashes of blinding lightening pierced the darkness. We were in the wrath of a tremendous storm that had moved from the south. It had hit with little warning, and now it was trying to blow us off the tree. Luckily enough, our tree was sheltered beneath taller trees, which protected us from the direct hit of the storm. The wind was blowing past us with all its fury. It was successful in toppling many giant trees to the forest floor.

Drenched and frightened, we were hanging on to our nest with all our might, taking our kids under our wings. Debris and leaves flew past us, as the storm raged unabated. The chilling rain continued. We were feeling completely terrified, humble and insignificant in the face of such power.

Finally, the storm passed beyond us. We were too wet to move our wings. It was still raining lightly but the winds and lightening had stopped.

Miserable, wet, and chilled to the bone, we were too tired even to check out if our little ones were alright beneath our wings.

After the rain had stopped, dark clouds continued to obscure the sun, which suddenly burst through them and was seen as a soft spinning disk of silver. Finally, the sun broke through the clouds, in its full splendor, and with it, returned the warmth we needed to restore our strength and our hope to survive. Still shivering in our wings, we emerged from the tree and fluffed our wings.

My little ones were shivering in fear, their little beaks trembling. The storm and rain has scared them out of their skins. I gently pecked them. "No more fear, Honey," I said to assure them. "The storm is over."

The Sun was shining bright again. Soon we were warm enough. I was sad noticing the broken nest of our neighbors. But we're all safe now. A sigh of relief came. Just then I noticed the little robin fallen on the ground. He fell on the ground and died during the storm. Oh God! I felt so sorry for the poor little one. How sorry his mom must be. I must go and meet her now.

However, I was not finding my strength to fly. I felt as if every ounce of blood has gone out of my body, I was so thoroughly shaken at the scene. What if this would happen to any of our kids! I shook my head and sat dazed. This incident cast a deep gloom over us, and I could not find my cheerful note to sing for a few days.

 ೮३ ৪০

It has been quite a few days till the storm had shaken our forest colony. The weather is warm and sunny now. There is not a trace of cloud in the sky. I was sitting on a lower branch of my Pine tree. My human friends didn't come the last few days. I was missing them.

Suddenly I saw Emma and Asher coming towards my tree. "How are you, Buddies? I missed you!" I squeaked in delight.

But when they came near, I noted something unusual. Emma's hairs were disheveled, eyes swollen. Asher was looking shaky too. I was at my wit's end. "What happened, Dear?" I asked as I flew down to sit upon Emma's shoulder.

Emma started sobbing. Little Asher heaved a deep sigh and his rosy lips trembled. I was almost moved to tears too.

"Dear Birdie, dad had to join the army for the impending war. He left us today," Emma whispered, as if to herself.

"War! What is a war?" I squealed in panic. She didn't understand what I said, but kept her soft hands on my feathers to caress me.

After they left, I suddenly remembered those men I noticed the other day. They must have something to do with the thing they called "war"! It must be a bad thing, because it made my friend's dad leave his family. Those peculiar fellows are bad people. I knew it. I knew it. My mind again raced with its ominous foreboding.

I flew across the valley to look around. I found those people, now larger in number, carrying some barrel like things. They looked like fighters. They were moving swiftly. Some of them were busy digging the ground. I noticed some suspicious looking big wheeled vehicles. I stopped for a moment, and flew over to get a closer look. With machine like precision they were carrying out their jobs. What the hell are they bent upon doing? I wondered why they must make our life so terrifying. We are just peace-loving harmless little birds and my friends, those mountain people, are simple peace loving folks too.

I was dismayed not to understand anything about their intention. But I must go back to my nest now. It's a long while since I left my little ones alone.

PART FIVE

I was feeling a little down today. I decided to visit Yashir. As I flew across his orchard, I found him sitting silently on a mat on his verandah.

He welcomed me in his usual loving manner. "Ah, welcome, Coco! Come, sit here," he said. "Where had you been these days? How are you doing? How's your family? I was so worried about you… you know, the thunderstorm…?"

"I'm fine, thank you," I chirped. "My family managed to do well during the storm, but the poor little Robin died, you know."

"Oh God!" he closed his eyes. "I am so sorry to know this. May God bless his soul!" We were silent for a few moments.

"I'm so glad that you are safe. Thank God," he said, opening his sparkling eyes.

"Did you learn about the war, Yashir?" I asked abruptly, having no clear idea about what it means.

His smile vanished. He looked distant and somber.

"Yes, Coco," he said slowly.

"It means a fight, right?" I asked smartly.

"A War is more than just a fight, Honey," he said. "It's not what you birds know as 'fight'. Humans possess dangerous weapons and bombs at their disposal. Wars destroy hundreds of innocent lives."

"Innocent lives!" I was alarmed. "Why? What harm have your people done?"

"Nothing," he said. "Humans engaged in the war are blind, Coco. They don't see what they do." Yashir sounded disturbed. His head dropped on his shoulder.

"Why does a war at all happen, Yashir?"

"The main causes of war are either territorial rights or narrow religious sentiments," Yashir said in a low voice.

"War is a fight between two immature super egos, each trying to prove its own supremacy over other.

Each side has its own justification, own agenda, own self-interest. They don't bother about the loss of innocent lives."

I was speechless in horror.

"War means that the stronger side attacks while the weaker ones defend; right?" I said, in an effort to come to a conclusion. "So the attacking side must be the wrong-doers."

"Very often quite the contrary," Yashir smiles piteously. "Most often the more fearful people are on the attacking side, as they say, 'attack is the best defense.' So the conclusion is not so simple, Honey."

"Do you mean to say that only insecure and fearful people are engaged in war?" I was stunned.

"Sure! Those who are hungry for power and want to lord over others are followed by fear and insecurity," he said. "But they utilize common people, brave, innocent people, to achieve their ends. I'm talking of the common soldiers, you know, the ones that are mere pawns in the game.

61

Simple innocent people like Emma's dad become victim of the fear, insecurity and lust for power of the few masterly minds that plot the wars."

"Very bad," I said dejectedly. "We birds too have differences among us. But we seldom kill each other."

"But those people are not to blame. They are immature and unconscious," Yashir said, sighing deeply. "And often they declare war to defend a right cause."

"Really?" I said. "But then, everybody should have the right to defend a right cause, Yashir," I chirped in confusion.

"True, but that will not solve the problem, Coco," Yashir said emphatically. "War is never a solution. It can't be. It will only breed more hatred, and more war."

"I understand," I said in dismay. "But should we not protest against a wrong act?"

"Sure, you should, but always at a higher level," he said. "If you protest on a lower level, you will either be a party to a war, or you'll be a victim of the war. You're a little bird. You can shout, or you will die. Protest should be made at the higher level."

"What do you mean by protesting on a higher level?"

"Protest must be done in a nonviolent way, by educating and awakening the consciousness," he said. "Healing the collective consciousness is the highest objective. Only that can bring permanent peace by erasing divisions and intolerance from the face of earth."

"Division and intolerance…?" I echoed his words, unable to understand the import.

"Yes," he said with a sigh. "Division and intolerance are the root causes of war."

"How's that, Yashir? I don't see any divisions," I cheeped in.

"We humans are talented beings, you know!" Yashir said, with pun in his voice. "We have superior and inferior nations, we have the first, second and the third worlds; we have created innumerable divisions in the name of colors, races and religions. We have divided the earth and humankind, and even the God in so many ways, you can't even imagine."

"But I know of only one world, Yashir. It is our world. How can there be so many worlds within one world?" I asked, befuddled.

"There is, little Birdie. You won't understand," Yashir insisted. "Incredibly intelligent that we humans are, we have managed to divide the earth and the sky too, and now we're bent upon destroying our own kind! By our irresponsible action, we are endangering the other species too." Anger, sarcasm, pity and desperation mingled in his heavy voice.

"This is not good," I shook my head in disbelief. "Something must be done about it."

"Sure!" he said. "We must do something about it."

"Can't your prophets and religions do anything about it?" I asked tentatively, remembering my little friends, who are very devout and steadfast in their religious vow.

"They often fight and declare war against one another, in the name of religion, and in the name of their prophets, you know!" he said, laughing aloud. "They compete with each other, trying to establish their supremacy."

"Oh my God!" I was shocked. "Why do they compete?"

"Because they are immature!" he said, shaking his head. "They don't understand that we are not here to compete, but to learn, evolve and excel. We are not here to make divisions in the name of prophets and religions. We are here to encompass the world with love and light."

"What religion do you believe in, Yashir?" I couldn't contain my curiosity. Yashir was silent for a moment. I believed I had asked him a question that is too personal. "I – I mean, what is your view on religion?" I reframed my question.

"I am free from the illusion of the religions, Coco," he said, smiling. I like the glint in his eyes. "I believe in the deeper goodness of every being," he continued. "My religion is to see the light and rainbow in every living being. My religion is developing deep faith in my inner being."

"So, you don't believe in a formal religion, Yashir. Do you?" I asked.

"You're right," Yashir said. "Religions often turn out to be like stagnant water, dirty and stinking. They need continuous evolution."

"I thought religions help you to become a better human being."

"Well," Yashir proceeded to explain. "Essentially religions contain many good teachings, you know. But over time they become narrow and parochial. Unfortunately, they often become the tool for exploiting innocent people."

"But you certainly believe in God, Yashir. Don't you?" I asked nervously.

"God is closer to me than anyone on this earth, Coco!" Yashir closed his eyes, and an unearthly light shone on his countenance, as if, he was transported to a different space. I was unfamiliar with this Yashir so far. But I was admiring the serene silence and profound peace he was radiating. I was actually imbibing the peace.

"God is the soul of my soul, the light of my eyes, the flow of my breath," he said again after a while, without opening his eyes. "But God does not need a religion for me to worship him. Religions, dogma and rituals are just obstructions, you know, for worshipping God in the sacred shrine of your heart."

I was feeling palpable peace in his presence. "God, without a religion sounds a wonderful idea, Yashir!" I chirped in delight. "It makes our relationship with God more meaningful and more personal."

"You are more mature than many humans I know, little darling," Yashir said opening his eyes. "Humans are still not mature enough to live and worship God without the layer of a religion or a sect. Most of them need an agent, and a society to adore God."

"But what do your religions give to the people?" I was curious.

"Unfortunately people forget the essence of the religions, and keep them busy with the peripherals," Yashir said with a sad smile on his lips. "For most humans, religions give them a social identity, a shelter to a guilty heart, and a promise of a glorious after-life, but they don't see that there is no greater religion than compassion, love and understanding towards God's creatures on the planet."

"Does God prize the soul that has a compassionate heart?" I was curious once again.

"Sure!" Yashir asserted. "A compassionate heart can bring peace in this world, and only a compassionate soul can have a glorious after-life."

This was a great revelation! I was happy to know this. However, I persisted with the questions in my mind.

"But Yashir, won't the soul become dry without a religion to hold on to?"

"No, if you know how to nourish your soul with the seeds of compassion, love and understanding," he said. "Your soul will be ever nourished and refreshed if you feed your soul with the knowledge of the interconnectedness of all lives and trust the God of sacred oneness."

I loved to drink his wisdom. My little feeding bowl was full, almost overflowing, and I drank to my heart's content.

"Thank you, for assuaging my doubts," I said in a grateful heart. "There is one last question, Yashir."

"It was my pleasure, Honey," Yashir gently smiled.

"I've seen my little friends joyfully celebrating during their religious festivals," I said a little hesitantly. "Will the life without a religion have any celebration left in it?"

I thought I have cornered my friend with a tough question. But he was unperturbed.

"Every new day, every little moment is a celebration of the spirit, Coco, "Yashir said. "Your life will be full of celebration if you learn to celebrate life with small things."

"Can we celebrate with small mundane things, Yashir?" I was a little confused.

"Sure!" Yashir looked ecstatic. He rose from his seat and facing the mountain in the east he turned the palms of his hands toward the sky. "God's signature exists on everything on this existence, Coco," he said, almost whispering the words under his breath. "Celebration is worship. Celebrate your eating, celebrate your drinking and celebrate your breathing. Celebrate your uniqueness, and celebrate your creativity. Celebrate the blessings of the moment."

I felt blessed to be taught this amazing wisdom. The doubt of my mind was cleared.

"Thank you, Yashir," I said humbly. "I'm learning important life lessons from you. I'll come again tomorrow."

"Just a moment, little darling," Yashir said. He moved towards his kitchen. He came back with a cupcake. He offered it to me. "I know this is your favorite. I've made some today, but forgot all about it in course of our conversation."

"The cake is delicious! Thank you," I said, tasting a little. "Please let me take some for Chico," I said, as I was busy nibbling it.

"Sure!" Yashir said, beaming in joy. "Take as much as you can, and come back tomorrow to have the rest of it. You can also bring Chico along with you. I haven't seen him for quite a while."

"Sure!" I said, and flew to my nest with a big piece on my little beak. I was only afraid of the Ravens. They are scarcely seen here, but they are a very greedy bunch. They fight for food and often snatch away foods from others. What a shame! However I didn't meet them on the way. Chico was delighted to have the piece of cake. He shared some with the kids.

ଔ ଛୋ

Today there was a marriage in the village. Marriage always means big feast and plenty of foods. Many of our feathered neighbors were visiting the village several times for foods. I found the delightful twittering of the starlings on my way to Yashir's home. Today Chico was with me too.

I told him that my friend Yashir has invited him. He delightfully accompanied me. As we arrived at Yashir's place, we found him sitting with closed eyes, meditating. We sat silently before him on his veranda.

After a while, Yashir opened his eyes and a broad smile adorned his face.

"Welcome home, Chico!" he said. "When did you two come?" That is his style. He'll make you at home in no time. I translated to Chico what he said, and Chico chirped his thanks to him. It had been a few days since Chico took interest in learning human languages. But he is still a novice in the skill. So, I have to often translate the words of Yashir to him, when they meet.

Yashir brought the cupcake, and we finished it gladly. Chico thanked him again, and prepared to leave with a big bite on his beak for the kids. He flew swiftly. They were alone in the nest.

"He's a very responsible bird," said Yashir, appreciatively looking at Chico as Chico rose up above the sky.

"Yes, Yashir," I said, "He takes a lot of care of the kids."

"Now Yashir, if you please agree to teach me," I said humbly, "I want to learn more about the important things we were discussing yesterday,"

"Sure, Coco!" he said. "Go ahead and ask what is in your mind."

"I'm still bothered with the question, you know," I muttered hesitantly.

"Yes?" Yashir looked up towards me.

"You said religions have little to do to bring peace on earth. Then what is the way?" I asked. "Will the idea of a peaceful world be elusive forever?"

Yashir remained silent for a while. He was probably thinking of the way to explain it to me.

"If religions can't bring peace on earth, Yashir," I persisted, "what is the way to bring peace on the earth?"

"Healing the collective consciousness is the only way to bring permanent peace on the planet," Yashir said at last. He looked serious.

"Healing the collective consciousness?" I repeated after him, unable to understand the import of his words.

"Yes, Coco! The Collective consciousness of the planet is sick with thought vibrations of fear, insecurity, aggression, un-forgiveness and crude intolerance," he said, thoughtfully. "It has been fragmented with violence and divisive thoughts. We need to heal it, make it whole. People invest huge amount for war arsenals but unfortunately very little for awakening the human consciousness."

"Are you sure that the sickness of our collective consciousness is solely responsible for war?" I was still trying to grasp the idea.

"Yes!" he said. "It's true. Our collective consciousness shapes the actions of us, the earthlings."

"Will you please elaborate on the point further?" I begged.

"Sure," he said. "War happens when the collective consciousness is fragmented, fearful, and directionless. War will stop when the light of awareness and compassion will heal the fragmentation."

"Healing means making it whole, right?" I chirped in delight to be able to grasp the idea.

"Right! You are an intelligent and wise bird." Yashir smiled. I almost blushed at the praise of my wise friend and guide, whom I admired the most on earth. However, there were still some doubts left in my mind.

"So, we need to work for healing the soul of humanity," I said thoughtfully. "But Yashir, how can a small bird like me, or a single person like you can heal the collective consciousness?" I asked.

"Good question!" Yashir beamed in joy to have a sincere student in me. He proceeded to explain in an effort to make it easily graspable by my little brain.

"You see, I, you and every sentient being belong to the collective consciousness," he said. "Our individual minds are parts of the collective consciousness. Our individual minds actually join together to form the collective consciousness. Do you follow me?" Yashir paused, looking expectantly upon me.

"Sure, Yashir! It's clear like daylight," I said.

"Good!" Yashir was happy to drive the point home. "Now, you know why and how each of us is responsible for the sickness or wholeness of the collective consciousness."

I was quietly listening to, actually gulping down this new wisdom.

"Our mind acts in three ways, you know: it acts like a generator, a receiver and a broadcasting station," Yashir continues.

This wisdom was entirely new to me. I let out a screech of wonder. "You mean to say that my mind works in this way too?"

"Yes, Coco!" Yashir smiles. A strange light glowed on his eyes. "Our mind acts like a generator. It generates fresh thought vibrations," he continued. "It also acts like a receiver, almost like an antenna that catches the existing thought vibrations floating in the collective consciousness."

I was speechlessly listening to him, admiring his wisdom. Yashir was noticing my silent expression of amazement. "Do you follow me, Birdie?" he asked again.

"Sure!" I said. "This information is a bit too much for me, though, to digest."

"I understand," Yashir said empathetically. "For now, just listen to me, Coco. You'll understand in time." Yashir placed his hand over my feathers. I feel safe and at home with him.

"Please tell me more," I said.

"Thoughts are vibrations, Coco," he said. "Whatever thought our mind generates or attracts, it vibrates with the same, in the process, generating and broadcasting in the environment multiple vibrations of similar nature."

"Wow! I now understand why generating positive thoughts are so important," I squeaked in delight. "The world is desperately in need of positive thought vibrations."

"You are a fast learner, Coco." My guide looked happy with my understanding. "You're right. When we are unconscious, we often catch the existing fearful thought waves, the thought waves of anger, division or aggression that float in the collective consciousness," he concluded.

"The more people vibrate in those negative vibrations, the more disharmonious vibrations are created, right?" I said, happy to get the idea behind it.

"Right, Coco." Yashir nodded. "And those disharmonious vibrations are radiated in the collective consciousness, making it sicker. It almost works with a viral effect."

I was dazzled with this wisdom. "I see now, Yashir, why the collective consciousness of our planet is so sick. Most people are living their lives very unconsciously."

"Yes, Dear. Unconscious and semi-conscious people catch the disharmonious vibrations, like anger, hatred, violence or depression. Their minds vibrate in tune with them, and in the process generate more disharmonies in the world," Yashir said. "People need to be more and more conscious, so war, the fruit of darkness will be driven out of the world for good."

He remains silent for a moment, absorbed in deep thought.

"We need to heal the soul of humanity," he said again after a while.

"Can we help the situation by praying for peace?" I asked curiously.

"Unfortunately not," Yashir quipped.

"Why?" I was surprised beyond my wit.

"No amount of prayer for peace can remove wars from the face of earth, Coco," he said emphatically. "Because, more often than not, such prayers stem from fear, and they only succeed in generating more fearful vibrations."

"Oh my God! That defeats the purpose," I quipped. I was stunned to know this.

"Yes," he said, and a strange light glowed in his eyes. "People seldom understand this. Prayers more often than not stem from fear, and such prayers do more harm than good. Only the prayer of a peaceful, relaxed and thankful heart can do any good."

"Does a thankful heart have any need to pray?" I asked uncertainly.

"You are right!" he said. "Gratitude itself is the highest form of prayer. The silent and peaceful heart is the fittest shrine of God."

"Then how can we do something to heal the collective consciousness, Yashir?" I came back to the point, inspired. "I'll do everything I can, to play my part in healing the soul of humanity. I'll do everything to ensure peace on our lovely earth."

Yashir smiled seeing my earnestness. "I am happy, dear, that you come forward to work for peace on earth. The collective consciousness will be healed by the light of love, understanding and compassion," he said.

"Do you mean to say that we need to practice consciously generating and cherishing such positive thought vibrations?" I asked.

"Sure! You are smarter than I thought!" he said lightheartedly, ruffling my feathers.

"But Yashir, does the individual thought of love, peace and compassion have such power to heal those stony hearts?" I said, referring to those warring people.

"It has, dear," he said. "Thoughts are like the powerful seeds of a fig tree. How tiny the seeds are, yet, how powerful? Have you seen a tree growing on a stony mountain?"

"Sure, I did," I quipped.

"Did you notice how they expand their roots on the mountain by cracking the stones slowly but inevitably?" He asked again.

"Sure. Now I understand the power of our tiny thoughts," I chirped in delight. "Our positive thoughts can indirectly benefit the whole planet. What a fabulous thing to know, Yashir! Thank you."

"It's my pleasure, little birdie. I'm glad that you can grasp this knowledge," Yashir said, as his bright eyes shone brighter. "But, I want to share with you the most secret wisdom regarding this."

"What's that, Yashir? Please tell me," I asked keenly.

"The highest type of practice in awakening the consciousness is touching the pristine ground of sacred silence, where just a pure intention can bring a miracle," he said. "Just an intention can begin the process of healing the collective consciousness."

"Really!" I quipped in delight. "Just an intention!"

"Yes, Coco," he whispered. "Just as a ray of the sunshine can pierce through the darkness, a pure intention can awaken the collective consciousness, when it comes from the ground of sacred silence."

It sounded true. If we are armed with the light of love, compassion and understanding, one day the shadow will be gone and the Sun will shine bright in its majesty. I could almost see the ray of light emerging from the ocean of love piercing the darkness of collective unconsciousness. Like a phoenix, consciousness will rise from its deep slumber.

"Yashir, one day we'll succeed in awakening the collective consciousness, and peace will reign for ever." My words echoed my thoughts.

"Sure, it's a monumental job, though. It will take time," he said slowly. "Sit silently and awaken the sacred silence in your heart. If our intention is pure and consciousness is crystal clear, success will follow."

"I'm with you, Yashir, and I'm sure Chico will be with us too. We'll walk the way together," I said in a committed voice, with my head held high, proud to be the part of a grander purpose of existing on the planet.

"Sure, Coco," said Yashir. "We'll walk the path together. Many will join us along the way. Slowly, but surely the collective consciousness will be awakened one day. By our concerted effort, the earth will be saved."

Yashir remained silent for a while, and then he said again, "We may have to sacrifice our lives. But our effort will not go in vain."

"How can we help the earth, Yashir, if we die?" I asked in dismay.

"Death is not the end, Honey. We are deathless beings. Death is the beginning of a new life in a new world," he said, caressing my feathers.

"So, nothing is lost in death?" I asked in delightful astonishment.

"Nothing is lost in death, except some trivial possessions and some unreal fantasies. The next-life is just the extrapolation of this life," he said. His words sounded firm and confident. "If this life is full of love, caring, joy and celebration, next life will also be like that. Our effort will not go in vain."

"Sure. Our effort will not go in vain," I repeated after him. I felt uplifted and happy. Now I was a bird with a purpose— with a single purpose in my life.

That is: to awaken the collective consciousness; to bring peace on earth, for the sake of all lives on earth, for the sake of the future generations of humans and birds and animals.

I flew to my nest, singing in joy. I wanted to share with Chico whatever I learned today. He is a noble soul too. I'm sure he will appreciate this, and together we'll fly the path of light.

PART SIX

A pall of gloom has descended on the valley and the mountains. Nobody is at peace nowadays. Men are leaving to join the army. Families are distraught. A shadow of impending disaster is hovering over the mountain. Food has become scarce too. We don't get our pieces of breads. We have to depend solely on the bugs and worms in the field.

One day I flew over the mountain to the other side to visit my friends. To my horror, I found them much distressed. Emma and Asher have become almost skinny in these few days. I found Asher quarreling over a piece of bread, and his mother beating him. I saw Emma crying. Her mom was holding them tightly near her bosom. She was helpless, being left alone with her little kids. I wished, I could wipe her tears with my tiny wings. I could not contain my tears as I flew back to my nest.

Everywhere in the village, I found broken families, with their main bread-earners leaving for the war. Those alien army recruited manpower from the local tribesmen.

I flew to my nest and rested on the topmost branch of my tree to ponder about the situation. I was feeling dejected, but there was a consolation. I learnt to dream of a better world, a world where our kids will breathe in peace.

Soon I brushed away my gloom. I held fast to my vision. I could almost see it materializing. I saw myself lovingly embracing the whole world with my wings, like I covered my kids under my wing. I dreamed of a world with no more wars. I wished I could really enlarge my wings to embrace the whole world with my love and light. I became immersed in my dream. I dreamed to breathe in the clean, refreshing smell of the forest again. I dreamed for a world where no gun might be lawfully fired at any of God's creatures.

ೂ ಐ

This part of the mountain is rocky and bare. I was taking rest on a cliff on the mountain, happily dreaming of my world of peace, when suddenly a loud sound pierced the quiet of the surrounding. I was not sure what it was, but an uncomfortable trickle of fear made its way slowly down through my spine.

Then I found men trampling on the ground. The earth trembled, and dust rose from the ground as their heavy boots stomped on the earth. They were not the village tribes I knew. They were carrying something in their arms. Fire! They were carrying fire arms!

Oh my God! What the hell are they bent upon doing? I thought. With a loud explosion detonating behind me, I was terrified as a second loud blast shattered the silence of the jungle. The bullets were cracking viciously all around. Suddenly, I was afraid.

I was flying across the mountain. I was flying for my life! I was just looking for a shelter. They were firing from above too.

They wanted to break the sky in to pieces! Oh God, they don't know what they are doing.

I dived down to the ground to take shelter in a bush. As I crawled into the bush, I suddenly remembered my children in the nest. Oh God! What are they doing there alone? A trickle of fear ran through my spine. In frantic pace I flew to my nest panicked, and sighed deeply to find them safe. I spread my wings to take them under my wings.

ॐ ॐ

The last few days had been tough. I had started patrolling to and fro from the village to my nest. I was concerned about the welfare of my village friends as well as the wellbeing of my feathered colony. I saw worries in the eyes of my neighbors. The blue Magpies were constantly making loud fearful noises. Sometimes it unsettled my nerves too. But I took resort to my dream of a world full of peace. I started dreaming of taking the whole world within the peaceful orb surrounded by my wings. My dream became my only consolation during these trying times.

It was just another gloomy day today that drained my energy and clouded my happiness. My anxiety has gotten the better of me. Nothing new happened there though. First thing after feeding my kids, I decided to visit the village today. I was worried about my friends — little Emma and Asher, and the good old Yashir. I darted out of my nest and hovered for a moment deciding where to go first.

First I flew to my little friends. I landed on a tree near their cottage to watch for a few minutes. I became suspicious by what I found. An alien soldier was conversing with Rihana, their mom. Rihana was nodding her head on both sides, evidently disagreeing to what the soldier said. In order to listen to their conversation, I flew nearer to sit on a wooden pole in their courtyard. Apparently the guy was trying to persuade the young lady to cook for them and take the food in their camp in lieu of good prices. But I was appalled as my birdie sense was foreboding of something evil, which I myself didn't clearly understand.

I went chirping on, to forbid her going there. But she didn't understand my warning. However, to my relief, Rihana didn't agree to the man's proposal at first. But at his persistence she finally gave in. She needed to feed herself and her little ones, I knew.

I wanted to fight the fellow off. But there was little I could do. I hovered in front of him and chirped at him, and then flew down on his head, trying to scratch it. I was just successful in making him startled for a while. But then he brushed me off, lighted his cigar, and took his seat on their veranda, thumping his boots on the ground to shake the dirt off his shoes.

I ventured off to find my little friends. They were on the meadow looking after their sheep and cattle. I flew over them hurriedly.

"Friends, go back home immediately," I said. "A dangerous person is persuading your mom to go with him. Please prevent her!"

But they couldn't understand me. What should I do now? Anxiety for her safety got the better of me. I was at my wit's end. Then I thought of flying to Yashir.

"Let's go and stop the young lady," I said to him.

He became grave. "Will she listen to me?" He said, but agreed, nevertheless, to go to her. He slipped in to his ragged gown and took his stick, and started walking towards their cottage. As we approached their hut, Rihana was about to leave with the soldier.

The lady was utterly surprised to see Yashir, because he seldom visited the village.

"How are you uncle Yashir?" She said.

"I'm fine. Please wait a minute, Rihana," Yashir sounded serious. "I need to tell you something."

"I'm in hurry now, uncle. Please! I'll come back within an hour."

"No. Listen. It's urgent," he said.

The young lady narrowed her eyes. "What's it?"

"Please don't go with this rogue. It won't be good for you," Yashir said in a low voice. "They are dangerous."

"But I have two little children to feed, uncle," she said. "You know their dad has departed for the war. There is no news of him so far. How do I sustain my family?"

"True. We'll find some way," Yashir insisted. "But don't go with this man."

They were talking between them in some ancient dialect, which the soldier didn't understand. But he grew impatient and suspicious.

"Hey! What's going on here?" He said in a hoarse tone, coming a few steps forward.

"We're sorry, but she can't go with you, young man," Yashir said in a quiet but firm tone. "She has a family to look after."

The soldier looked violent. It made me alarmed.

"It's none of your business, Old dog. Understand?" He said scornfully, and coming near Yashir, pushed him aside with such a force that my poor friend stumbled on the ground. I inhaled a sharp breath and struggled for another.

Yashir didn't move his eyes off the soldier, though. There was something in his eyes that unnerved the soldier.

"I - I'm sorry." The soldier mumbled in a low voice, as if to himself. "I mean to say that I have nothing against you, Sir. She agreed to go with me, for cooking our food... We'll offer her a good remuneration...," he blabbered uncertainly.

Yashir didn't reply. He just got up on his feet, brushing the dirt off his shoulder.

Rihana was hesitant. She stood frightened and perplexed, with the food carrier still in her hand. The soldier stepped forward, grabbed her hand and dragged her along. Now she possibly knew what blunder she had committed, by agreeing to go with this brute. Thoroughly frightened and confused, she went along unwillingly, looking back again and again. But it was too late. There was possibly nothing we could do now.

I flew down to Yashir. "Are you hurt, dear friend?" He looked quiet and unperturbed by the assault upon him.

"I'm alright, Coco. I feel just a little pain in my elbow," he said, brushing the dirt from his ragged gown. "But I'm really worried about Rihana and her children, you know."

101

I kept company with him for a while, and then I took leave from him to fly back to my little ones. Yashir said he would be there to assure the children, and wait till they return with their cattle.

Today was an eventful and tiresome day for me. I was upset and worried. I needed rest. My daily routine had been disrupted. On my way back to my nest, I stopped at my favorite spot to have a drink. I flew back to my nest to rest for the evening. Tomorrow I'll start all over again.

ଔ ଛ

Today morning, as the Sun went up high on the mountain, I ventured off to their home. I found Emma and Asher sitting on the ground utterly exhausted from crying the whole night. There mom hasn't returned.

I knew this would happen. She would never return. My mind started chirping again. I felt upset and irritated. I tried to console them in vain. I flew to Yashir to report it to him. He was shocked. He shook his head in disbelief. Immediately he started from his home to take those orphaned kids in his caring shelter.

My heart was broken. My little friends were homeless orphans now. War had robbed them off their beloved parents. I know how badly they needed Yashir now. He is so loving and caring. I thanked him for being so kind to my friends. I flew back to my kids, thoroughly shaken at the turn of the events.

The hell broke loose in the afternoon. This was indeed a dark day. The firing started again on the mountain. Bullets were cracking overhead and thudding into the ground. Missiles were flying. We were hiding in our nest among the dense leaves.

Then came the terrifying sound of the massive blast. Once again, another one! The monstrous roar of the massive blast deafened our ears. It came from the direction of the village. After a while, it was suddenly quiet once again. But there was a storm of dust all around. The sky was dark with smoke. We could hardly breathe in the suffocating smoke in the air.

Evening came down, signaling the end of a horrific day. I sat beside Chico, covering our kids with my wings. I was utterly exhausted and confused. Why do humans love killing themselves? Don't they love their children? The war results in so many lost homes and broken families. Don't they see that?

We spend the night with the nightmare of the war haunting us.

The Sun rose in the east taking away the gloom of the night. But it was not like the other mornings. The air was still heavy with the smell of gun-powder. The sky had taken a strange pale gray hue. Our hearts were heavy too. Our feathered colony was aghast in fear. Only some of them were twittering in low notes.

I was frightened too. My song had left me. In low hushing voice I was brooding and mourning for my village friends. God knows how they are doing. The ground below was trampled by the soldiers. I was afraid to fly down to the ground. Luckily, I found a few bugs on the branch, and with them I fed my babies. I didn't feel like eating.

I decided to have my breakfast at Yashir's home. That was the place I badly needed to go now. Last evening the sound of blast came from the direction of the village. I was worried about them. I took a flight across the mountain to the village.

In the middle of the sky I was stalled in terrible panic. Humanity has lost all senses. They have just gone crazy. Oh my God! What a scene! The scene of carnage on the ground froze me on the sky. I trembled in sudden rage at the wanton barbarity of the humans.

I cried in anguish. You wretched humans, what do you gain by fighting? What do you fight for? Doesn't your God provide enough for your whole race to survive on earth?

What a shame that you fight and destroy lives on the earth. You are an intelligent race. When will you learn to respect the freedom of lives on earth?

God has endowed you with the power to create a beautiful world, and what have you done? I see an utter wastage of your God-gifted power, potential and intelligence. I cried in anguish. But I knew. I'm just a tiny mountain bird. No one was listening to me.

I found part of the village destroyed. Everywhere there was debris of what had once been beautiful huts throbbing with lives. I was appalled and ashamed at the scene of sheer mass destruction.

From up above the sky I smelled the stench of death. Few of the bodies were in one piece. They did not just die. They were scattered in death. Parts of the bodies were dispersed everywhere along the ground. I was transfixed on the sky fighting my nausea. I could almost hear their cries of horror and agony.

What harm did these peaceful villagers do? They had been guilty of no crime other than a desire to be left alone, and allowed to live their humble lives, planting, harvesting and tending their cattle. But the cruelty of the war had found them helpless, and extracted a deadly price from them.

I was shocked. My wings trembled. Did humans lose their sense? Did they really believe that they stood for what was right, good and true? Can any war really stand for what is right good and true?

Can murder of their folks be a solution to anything?

Oh God! Why are they so insane? How do they pride themselves to be the most intelligent being on the planet?

What I was looking at was all wrong. It was the loss of humanity and glorification of insanity. For the first time I realized that something had really gone terribly wrong with the humans.

My soul suffered at the scene of the human corpses. I felt sick. I couldn't take it anymore. I came down a little to find a jackal treading on the ground among the corpses.

They say, wars are fought for worthy causes, for the triumph of good over evil. How immature they sound! War, a weapon of mass destruction of life and environment, itself is the highest evil. What good can come out of the evil that war is? War is a sickness, a sickness of the human soul. War is the outcome of massive unconsciousness.

I was flying back to my home. I was in tears thinking of the little Emma, Asher and my beloved friend Yashir. God knows what happened to them. Tears blocked my eyesight. All my strength had left me. When I came very close to my nest, I heard that dreadful sound of bomb-blast again. Oh my God! They were firing from above. Looking above, I found two gigantic air vehicles spitting fire! Horrified, I flew to my nest to cover my kids.

PART SEVEN

But alas! I was too late. My children were dead, my nest broken. I couldn't cry. Perhaps my heart has become frozen. I felt massive holes in my heart. Will my soul ever heal?

I learnt from my friends that humans believe in God. They preach religion. But they kill God's creatures and take shelter under their religion. With all their prayers, incantations, and songs of salvation, the humans fight against one another. They pray to God to assist them to kill their brothers! The darkness of religion is darker than night, because treading on darkness, they believe that they are on light.

Alas! They do not know. So long as they enshrine the thoughts of hatred and revenge in their hearts, the sacred shrine of God can never find a place in their hearts.

Nations fight against one another in the name of justice. What justice do they seek by killing innocent people? Why do they fragment the earth and life in the name of anything? Can they divide the sky too? What utter foolishness!

We, birds, sing our sweetest song as we feel the boundless freedom of the unbounded sky. But the humans do not know the sacred sanctity of wholeness. They divide and fragment the existence in the name of egoistic mental constructs. They name those ideas as cast, sect, nationality, religion and what not... And they fight wars to protect those mental constructs. Perhaps we are wiser than them!

When will the humans be mature enough to live without a religion, without a nationality, without any labels to divide one another? When will they be mature enough to stop labeling themselves in the name of superior or inferior nations, in the name of class, caste, cult or color of their skins? Will they ever learn to live in the silent dignity of peace, love and understanding?

The warmongers don't understand so long as they remain hungry for war, for revenge, their soul will remain hungry. Only peace can appease the hunger of the soul.

We were flying through the forest in search of a safe sanctuary, when once again the silence of the forest was savagely interrupted by the sounds of bullets in the air. Two low flying air vehicles came down hunting each other. We narrowly missed clashing with their massive wings. But, just before we took shelter atop a dense Pine tree, my wing clashed against the window of another air vehicle. I felt a sharp pain shearing through the rearmost corner of my right wing. For a moment my senses numbed and I started falling.

Seeing me falling, Chico quickly slowed down and changed the angle of his wings. With a sharp turn of his wings, he came beside me and we finally landed on a bushy Oak tree. Overhead the air vehicles were spitting fire.

"Are you alright, Dear?" Chico whispered. I shook my head without saying anything. He had covered me with his wings the entire time the air vehicles were spitting fire. He ignored the bullets whining past his head and tearing bark off the trees nearby. My wing was aching. My body was shivering.

Am I dying?

We look in to the eyes of each other.

"Just in case I die today, I want to say, Chico, I love you," I whispered to him.

"I love you too, Dear," he said back. "But, don't worry. You'll be alright soon."

But I was scared. I was scared of death. I was scared to have to part from my mate.

"I am so happy that I could share this life with you, Chico." My voice almost choked in tears.

Chico brought his crest near mine and rested it on mine. A drop of tear fell from his eyes too. "Nothing can separate us, Darling," he whispered. "Not even death. Even if we die today, I'll meet you in the land of light."

"Sure!" I smiled. My pain eased. "In the land of light!" I whispered. I remembered the words of Yashir again. "Death is not the end. We are deathless beings," I smiled and relaxed in peace.

"Yes, death has no power over us!" Chico said, as a drop of tear sparkled at the corner of his eyes. "You are my best friend," he said. "Our friendship is rooted in one soul but dance in two bodies. The first day when I looked at you, you were a stranger, but suddenly you became my whole world. I can't imagine living without you."

"So true!" I said with a sigh.

I don't know if my days on earth are going to be over. Will I sing again? Will my song ever be heard on the valley again? Will I ever dance with the wind again? Will I ever spread my wings again under the azure sky?

I felt a deep anguish against those warring brutes who robbed me off my peace. But suddenly in the midst of this darkness, I had a moment of clarity. I remembered the words of my friend Yashir. "They are ignorant and unconscious. They can't see what they are doing." As soon as I remembered those words, my heart felt lighter and softer for those ignorant people. I was filled with profound compassion, with love for everything that exists, and I breathed in peace.

But my eyes seemed heavy. Deep slumber was coming down upon me. I let go of a sigh. "I forgive you, men — you, who are bent upon killing one another; you, whose bullet robbed me of my dear kids. I forgive you. My beloved earthlings, it is my earnest wish that you may come in to sense. I wish that you may learn to prize peace. I wish that you may learn to protect the dear earth and all its beings. I love you earthlings! I wish you good with my whole heart, even if I might have to depart from this abode." As I uttered this in my mind, suddenly my pain vanished and my heart became lighter. I suddenly felt that my wings were long enough and my heart wide enough to embrace the whole world.

Then a miracle happened. My heart took the form of a bright light and it started expanding. Slowly my whole being was shimmering with a bright golden white light. It was such an ecstatic feeling. I wanted to sing in joy. Lo! I could sing again. My song has become a melody of lucid light. I know that my song will spread far and near. It will touch the strings of many hearts, and flowers of thousand petals will blossom.

Now I realize that I don't need to move an inch to make my voice heard. I don't need to utter a word. My voice is perfect and my intention is pure. I know that it will touch the hearts and reach every corner of the world.

I was floating in to the lucid light of love. It was a magnificent land where not a trace of darkness existed. I found Chico, who had also been transformed in to a ball of lucid light that was expanding. We met, melted and merged, and we spread over the hills and dales. Our beings of light spread and spread... spread in the mountain, and hills and dales, in the rivers and on the sky, in the hearts of all beings, in the hearts of all birds, beasts and humans, in the hearts of friends and foes, melting the stony hearts, melting enmity, anguish and hatred, melting fear, jealousy and greed, erasing all mental divisions, separations and boundaries.

The beautiful light of love shone brighter and brighter and flowed to illumine the whole world, and took the whole world in its orb. I was utterly astonished and delighted, because this was exactly how I had dreamt of embracing the world with my wings. My world had turned to be perfect and whole. My dream came true. My delight and astonishment started melting in to a profound sense of peace. I surrendered my little self completely in to the bright luminous flow of golden light that spread in every corner of the universe.

I opened my eyes as a bright ray of light woke me up from my swoon. I couldn't think clearly. Is it heaven? Have I died? I looked around. Chico was there right after me anxiously looking at me. "How're you doing, Darling?" I heard him whispering. What a beautiful morning! The Sun was shining bright. So I am alive! I AM ALIVE!

My heart leaped in joy! Never in my life have I felt so happy just to be alive.

"I'm alright. Don't worry," I assured Chico. I was feeling just a little weak, and I felt a little heaviness in my right wing. The nightmare of yesterday is gone.

Just then I remembered him — my friend Yashir. There was a blast yesterday in his village. I don't know if he is still alive. My eyes glistened with tears. I don't find any courage left in me to face what I might have to see in my friend's place. But I must go. I must go to Yashir. God save him. Chico followed me without a word as I took off.

As we approached Yashir's cottage in trembling heart, my wings were dragging me down. I felt unsettled, worried and anxious. Finally I landed on an apple tree in his orchard, and looked around. I sighed in relief seeing him sitting on his veranda. He was looking towards the mountain with vacant eyes.

"Yashir!" I chirped in delight and flew to sit on his shoulder. "Thank God! You are alive!"

Chico landed beside him on his veranda.

"How're you two?" Yashir kept his hand upon my feathers, friendly smile lighting up his face. "I'm so happy that you are safe!" His voice sounded heavy.

"God is kind, Yashir, that we're alive," I whispered. A drop of tear blurred my eyesight. "I narrowly escaped death," I said. "There is still some pain in my wings and I am feeling weak too."

"Oh my God!" Yashir said. He took me on his lap and examined my wound. Then he put me down on the mat beside Chico.

"Just wait for a moment, Coco. Let me prepare some medicine for you," he said, and quickly disappeared inside his cottage. He returned after a while with two bowls in his hands. He placed the bowls beside us, and picked some leaves from a shrub growing on his courtyard. He rubbed them in his hands and mixed it in to one of the bowls.

"This herbal medicine will quickly heal you, Honey," he said, holding me carefully in his hands. He placed me on his lap with such care and compassion that I was moved to tears! Yashir noticed it. "Did I hurt you, Coco?" He asked.

"Not at all," I chirped. "You are so kind and so caring. I'm almost healed by your healing touch."

"These medicinal herbs from the mountain have wonderful healing qualities," he said. "I'll rub this paste in to your wound, and you'll be alright soon."

The herbal paste was cool and fragrant. After he rubbed those herbs in to my skin, almost instantaneously I was feelings much better. Then he put me down on the mat and placed the other bowl in front of me.

"What's in it, Yashir?" I asked.

"Drink this potion, Dear." Yashir said softly. "This will bring the strength back in to your body."

I drank it up in no time. Soon I was feeling great.

"I don't know how to thank you, Yashir," Chico said. He was delighted, observing me getting back the strength in my body.

"It was my pleasure, Chico. You two are very dear to me." Yashir said. "I spent the last night thinking of you two. How are your kids?"

Chico was silent. His eyes glistened.

"We couldn't save our kids, Yashir," I couldn't say any more. My voice choked in tears.

Yashir closed his eyes. "That's terrible news!" he said. "I'm so sorry. I beg forgiveness from you on behalf of my insensitive human brethren." He sighed deeply. He was looking really sad today.

"Please don't say so, Yashir. That breaks my heart," I said earnestly. "It's none of your fault, and they are ignorant, as you say."

"True," Yashir said. "They, those warring humans, are unconscious, Coco. They don't know how much suffering they are creating."

It is just then that I noticed little Asher and Emma coming from inside of his hut.

"How're you, Emma?" I chirped in delight. "I'm so glad to see you two safe here."

Emma smiled faintly, and they came to sit beside Yashir. I found little Asher unusually silent. He looked shaky and restless too. The poor one was still grieving the loss of his parents, I knew.

Yashir was looking sad and somber too.

"Listen little ones," he said in a deep voice. "You have come just in time. I have decided to leave this place. It's no longer safe. I have already talked to the villagers, those who are still alive."

"Leave this place?" I was alarmed.

"Yes, Dear. It's no longer safe here," Yashir said calmly. "You two, Chico and you are coming with me. Right?"

"What? I mean, okay... We birds can move anywhere, but," I gulped down a knot in my throat, "what about the villagers? Are they willing to leave this place?"

"Unfortunately not," Yashir said, frustration written on his face. "Many are so deeply attached to this place that they will rather die here than leave. But a few, a few young friends will follow me."

"But where will we go?" I asked, still dazed at the idea. There are so many memories, so many happy dreams here... Even the thought of leaving this place is painful.

"There is a green valley to the south of this place." Yashir said. "It's a few days walk from here. We'll move there, and begin from new."

"A new valley!" Chico said, puzzled. He was closely following our conversation.

"Yes, Dear." Yashir said. "We'll name it the Valley of Hope. There are plenty of fruit bearing trees. You can build your nest on one, and we'll take our cattle and sheep along with us. We'll build our new village."

"What will we do there, Yashir?" I said, still unable to come in terms with the idea.

"What are we doing here, Coco?" Yashir asked echoing my question.

I was silent for a while. It's true that life has become miserable here. "We are praying for the war to stop. We are hoping for a better future and dreaming of peace reigning on earth again," I said thoughtfully.

"Right," Yashir said. "We'll do just that there, in a better way. We'll work to heal the collective consciousness of the planet."

I remembered my trance of the land of light, when I fainted from the clash with the air vehicle. Was it a dream? Or, was it a vision of a new future? I don't know, but my heart felt ecstatic.

"Sure!" I chirped. "I am, I mean, we're coming with you."

"Definitely!" Chico agreed. "We'll follow you."

A group of young village folks entered Yashir's courtyard in the middle of our conversation. Women were carrying small bundles of clothes and utensils on their heads, and small babies on their backs. Men were carrying long sticks and holding reins of their cattle.

"We're ready, Yashir," A tall handsome boy came forward, and said. "Should we start now?"

"Sure!" Yashir said ardently. "Now! Now is the time, Adrian." Yashir blinked his sparkling eyes gazing at me.

Leaving the comfort of a known territory was not easy. I found tears in many of their eyes. It was scary to take that first step towards an unknown land. They were leaving behind their village, their neighbors, their land and their pastures, for an unknown destination. Their neighbors and relatives came to see them off. It was heart-breaking scenery.

Yashir stood before the crowd tall, calm and poised. He cleared his throat to address them.

"My friends, we are all set to begin our journey today," he said. "Leaving a known setting and venturing for the unknown requires no small courage, I know. But we can't just wait here for an impending death." He paused a little. There was dead silence, though all the eyes were set upon him.

"We have no other choice." Yashir said again. "You, those who decided to follow me, everyone belong to one family, from today. We are one family, with one intention and one single purpose. We are like the leaves of a tree. Separate on the top but connected at the root. This move will help all of us to grow as a person and enrich our life in unimaginable ways."

"We are scared, Yashir." A faint little voice said. It was Sophie, a cute teen standing in the middle of the front row.

Yashir looked at her eyes tenderly. "I understand, Sophie," he said affectionately. "But if we don't make the effort to step outside of our bubble, we'll perish here. There's life beyond the confines of our familiar village streets, fields and pastures, you know. Believe me, everything will be alright soon. Together we'll make it." Yashir paused. Sophie burst into tears. She ran forward and embraced Yashir. "I am broken and fragile. I need your help," she said. "I've lost my parents. I trust you'll lead us to a safe sanctuary." She sobbed into his massive chest. Like a loving father, Yashir gently patted on her head, murmuring consoling words in to her ears to calm her down. She looked assured and relaxed.

So we set off on a new journey for an unknown land, and unknown destiny. We started our journey, with the Sun at our left. Yashir is our leader. He is the wisest man in the village. People admire him for his wisdom. I felt proud to be his friend. The few people that dared to follow Yashir were wiser and more courageous than the rest, I know.

Our folks were walking together in a cue. Young men carrying sticks and reins of cattle were in the front part, women and children in the middle and stronger people were in the rear part of the team.

We were flying over them. I heard the call of my nest, the call of the valley, the call of the sky. But I have lost my voice. An unknown lump is formed in my throat. I tried to take a deep breath. Good bye dear valley, good bye my mountain, good bye my river! I love you all.

We are moving forward towards the valley of hope. We'll dream of a better earth there. We'll build a new nest, with new hopes in our hearts. But shall we be truly able to move past those nightmarish days of the past? Won't they haunt us for the rest of our lives?

Our hearts yearned for the peace, happiness, and prosperity of the olden times. Is it just a dream or a fantasy to believe that those conditions will ever again exist on the earth? Will we, this handful of us, be able to heal and repair the sickness of the collective consciousness? Clouds of thoughts haunted me.

After a few miles, we took some rest beside a mountain stream, and then resumed our journey again.

At Sunset, Yashir decided to make our camp under a bushy Oak tree on a large expanse. Three young men, Adrian, Johan and Bashar lit a fire, and the ladies joined together to cook meals.

After the dinner, everybody was sitting around Yashir. Chico and I were sitting on a branch right above his head. I swooped down to sit beside him. Yashir's face was beaming in the moonlight.

Covered under the blanket of moonlight, the earth, the mountain and the land was looking beautiful, unearthly. Everybody was silent, waiting for Yashir to open the conversation. He looked like a Yogi with his closed eyes. Slowly he opened up his eyes, and smiled at Emma and Asher who were sitting close to him.

"So, we have left behind our past," he said. "We have left behind our old land, old relations, old possessions and old memories, both good and bad."

"But Yashir," Adrian cleared his throat. "It is really painful to let go of those things, you know. We're all suffering within."

"I know," Yashir nodded. "We've lost our loved ones. It's not easy to forget the past. But that is the only way to live, Adrian. I mean, if you want to live an alert, intelligent and meaningful life, you must let go of the past."

"We have lost much, Yashir, but so long as we're alive, we need to move forward, right?" I intervened. "After all, life is a wonderful gift."

"Right." Yashir smiled at me. "You are a wise bird. Life itself is the most precious gift. Love is the most precious possession."

"We've already left the baggage of the past, Yashir, but memories are difficult to forget," Said Bashar. "Please teach us, Yashir, the way to live our new life."

"Live in the awareness of the moment, Bashar. Live in love." Yashir exhorted.

"How can we live in love, Yashir, when all the while hatred ravages our hearts?" Said Irfana, a young lady from the group. "We hate them who made us leave our land and killed our relatives."

Yashir nodded. His eyes glowed with a soft light.

"I understand your pain Irfana," he said. "But I beg you to forgive them. They are unconscious. They don't know what they are doing. They are blinded by their self-interest."

"How can I forgive them, Yashir?" Irfana started sobbing. "I had lost my sister in the war. I had to leave behind my old parents in the village to save my kids and my family. They were unwilling to leave the village at this old age, you know."

Johan, Irfana's husband placed his hand upon her shoulder to calm her down.

"I could have destroyed them, if it was in my power, Yashir." Adrian howled, closing his fists.

Yashir was silent for a moment.

"But that's just how a war begins, Adrian," he said slowly, after a while. "Hatred, revenge, bringing justice, there are many such reasons to start a war; you name it. But there is no end to it. Will it ever bring a solution? Will it leave our offspring a peaceful earth to breathe and live on? Just think for a moment."

Yashir's words created an electrifying effect on the folks. Adrian's head droops down on his shoulder, and Irfana suddenly stopped sobbing.

"True, Yashir, I get your point," Irfana said. "I want a peaceful earth for my children. I don't want them to suffer as I have suffered. But, is it ever possible?"

"Yes, Irfana, it's possible." Yashir's eyes shone. "True, today's realities are war, crime, hunger and sickness, to mention just a few. Yet there is reason for hope. With the help of God within us, we'll create a new consciousness, a new earth."

"But Yashir," Johan frowns. "Is it realistic to believe that a new earth is possible?"

"Was it realistic to believe that we could survive in the middle of the mass destruction that was going on in our village, Johan?" Yashir asked.

Johan kept quiet, but looked up to Yashir expectantly.

"We did it by taking alert and timely decision. With awareness, determination, intelligence and compassion, anything is possible, Johan," Yashir said again. "We must not give up. Every challenge comes with new opportunities. We need to move forward in the light of awareness."

"We are with you, Yashir." Said Teeber, a young lad. "But we're bothered with the past. It haunts us. Please show us the way."

"Past will cease to bother you, Teeber," Yashir said, a deep poise shining on his face, "if you learn to live in the moment."

"How do we live in the moment, Yashir?" Teeber asked.

"Well, Teeber, do you believe in God?" Yashir asked.

"Why? Sure, I believe in God." Teeber said hesitantly, trying to grasp the purport of this question.

"Do you believe that this wonderful creation is created by an unknown, unseen power, whom you may call your God?" Yashir asked again.

"We all believe that this forest, river, mountain, humans and animals are God's creation." Said Adrian.

"Then, henceforth treat this earth as holy ground," Said Yashir. "Live in the moment, admiring the beauty of the Nature. Looking at beauty in the world is the first step of purifying the mind. Know that you are living in the paradise, here and now."

"Please pardon my doubt, Yashir." Teeber said. "Is it not fooling ourselves to think that we are living in a paradise, while the reality speaks otherwise?"

"Doubts are welcome, Teeber, so long as you are willing to learn," Yashir said, with a glint in his eyes. "No, Teeber," he said again. "It is not fooling ourselves to think that we're living on the paradise. God wanted to create a paradise, and earth is that paradise. Nowhere in the Universe, there is so much life and beauty. In fact, it all depends on us. We are the gods and demons that can make the earth paradise or hell. The choice is ours to make."

"The choice is ours!" Teeber repeated after him.

"Yes, Dear. The choice is ours. We humans decide what to make of our earth, a heaven or a hell."

Yashir said. "When we live in love, in joy, in empathy, understanding and awareness, we live like a god, and the earth we tread upon becomes paradise. When we live in hatred, anger, greed, insensitiveness or unawareness, we behave like a demon, and make the earth hell."

"I have never thought it this way, Yashir. Thank you for this wonderful insight." Teeber said thoughtfully. "But the reality of war and agony…?" Teeber stopped in the middle of his sentence.

"What is reality, Teeber? Who creates the reality? It is we, our consciousness that creates the reality," Yashir said emphatically.

"I get your point," Adrian said. "We need to work to heal our consciousness."

"There you are." Yashir's eyes were shining bright. "Healing starts with us, and living in the moment heals. Live in awareness of the moment; live in love with Nature. Live in compassion. Only then you can consciously radiate peace."

"Please teach us more about living in the moment, Yashir." Irfana was earnest.

"Begin with Nature, Irfana. Let everything in this wonderful creation of God, bring you back to this moment." Yashir's voice became soft and mellow. "Earth is the holiest place in the Universe, loving the earth, and loving life is the way to generate positive vibrations.

"Find joy in every ordinary thing in your daily life, in the smell of fallen leaves, in the murmuring of the Pines, in the ions of the waterfalls, in the lights of the Sun, in the melting of the snow, in the blooming of the flowers, in the eyes of creatures, in the smiles of open hearts."

"Is it that easy to heal our hearts, Yashir?" Said Bella, a young girl sitting next to Irfana.

"Yes, Bella," Yashir said. His face lighted up. "It is easy, when you let go of the past and live in the moment, as I said."

"But Yashir," A voice came up from the end of the rows. Jerads, an arrogant looking young lad shrugged his shoulders. "All this sounds bullshit-mumbo jumbo. Actually I can't agree with what you say."

There was pin drop silence among the group. Yashir quietly looked up towards him without saying a word.

"I mean, we are just escaping like pigs, without taking any constructive step to solve the problem," Jerads grumbled, "and now you talk about forgiving them and healing our own consciousness! What good will it do?"

"So, do you have another solution?" Irfana snapped back. "Tell us. What's it?"

"If you think we are just escaping, why don't you just go back and try to solve the problem?" asked Bashar.

There was no answer. Jerads shifted uncomfortably in his seat. All the eyes were set upon him.

"You're trying to be smart, Jerads, while you are talking immaturely. What alternative did we have?" Adrian said in a voice of reproach. "We have trusted Yashir as our leader. We're sure he will lead us to the right path."

"Let him speak his mind, Adrian," Yashir said, "Let him unburden his heart."

"Don't get me wrong," Jerads murmured. "I was just thinking if our duty was to find a constructive solution to the problem, and - and I also wanted to punish those people."

"Whom will you punish, Jerads?" Yashir asked. "Do you know who are truly responsible for the war? Not the soldiers, not even the commanders. Know that the people, who planned the war in cool brain, are sitting far away from the war zone. They are beyond your reach, and they too are victims of the pain and sickness of the collective consciousness."

"Then what's the solution?" Jerads sounded impatient. "Can't we do anything about it?"

"The task is not to take revenge, but to repair the hearts. And only compassionate hearts can repair the wounded hearts," Yashir said in a firm but calm voice. "Our duty is not to punish people - but to awaken the consciousness. The people, who plotted the war, are also part of the collective consciousness. If we can not heal the collective consciousness, we can't transform those ignorant, unconscious and selfish people. Only a mass awakening can eliminate their evil motives. And to do that you, I and every one have to work. As a human being, healing the consciousness is our highest duty."

"But that goes over our heads, Yashir," Jerads said, fidgeting nervously. "We're small. We're too imperfect to follow such a grand and massive goal."

"That's where you go wrong, Jerads." Yashir said, shaking his head. "We are not small. Our hearts are wide enough and hands are long enough to embrace the world."

"But we can't deny that we carry the wounds within us, Yashir. You may be perfect, but I am not." Jerads sounded loud and edgy. "I have anger, I have hatred, I have jealousy. I carry the hurt of the death of my parents and my brother in the war." His voice broke.

"I understand your pain, Jerads," Yashir said softly. "That is why I said that healing and awakening starts at the level of individual."

"But I can never forgive those warring brutes," Jerad said, making balls with his fists, and knocking them on the ground.

"You can, Jerad, if you will. You don't know what amazing strength resides within you." Yashir said, looking straight in to his eyes. "Do you know what happens when our soul begins to awaken? Our eyes, our hearts and every cell of our body dance in celebration with the rays of compassion, awareness and love. We begin the joyful journey on the path of love. We see that we all are so deeply interconnected, we have no option but to love all."

"Love is just a word to me, Yashir," Jerads nodded his head in frustration. "I don't see any possibility of tasting it in this life again. Hatred is all that I carry."

Yashir remained silent for a while. "Sixty years back I myself lost my parents in another war, when I was only ten." He said slowly. "I too faced many challenges. I spent alone many dark nights that seemed to last forever. Do you know the pain of an orphan in an unfriendly world?"

Jerads was dumbfounded. "I - I never knew this…, I – I'm sorry, Yashir." Jerads stammered. "I thought you never knew the pain of separation from the loved ones."

Yashir smiled. It was a sad smile. I was feeling very sorry for my friend. Everybody was feeling sorry for him. We never knew he had such a troubled past. In spite of growing up in an unfriendly world, he has turned up to be a wonderful human being— such a caring, compassionate and wise person. I felt proud of him.

"I am really sorry, Yashir, for the way I behaved." Jerads said again. "If you could transcend your hurt in such a small age, I too probably can." The boy was back in his sense.

"It's alright, Jerads, to question new ideas, if you are open to learn." Yashir said in a candid voice. "Life throws challenges, and every challenge comes with rainbows and lights to conquer it," he said again.

"Did you never have negative thoughts, Yashir, about those people who killed your parents?" Jerads asked. He looked earnest.

"I was not born perfect, Jerads. In fact, perfection is something we're all striving for. I had experienced anger, hatred and frustration too," Yashir said in a distant voice. "But I've never allowed them to dominate my life, because life has taught me that negative thoughts never bring any solution. They only succeed to cloud our consciousness."

"You've been brave and strong, Yashir," Jerads said humbly. "Please show us the way to conquer the negative thoughts."

"Don't be caged by the negative thoughts. - Feel the freedom of the new opportunities. Think about the new generations and the new world, Jerads," Yashir said. "Let go of the past and focus on the present moment. Bring all your energy to create a wonderful present. It will heal your hurts."

"But how's that going to solve the problem of war, Yashir?"

"It will help to solve the problem of war, Jerads," Yashir said firmly. "You are a tiny part of the collective consciousness. When you heal yourself, a hole in the collective consciousness is repaired. And when you are healed, you are ready to take the next step. Then together we'll work to heal the collective consciousness of this planet, which is sick with the thoughts of division and hatred, anger and revenge. When the collective consciousness is healed, war will stop forever."

"This sounds familiar!" I chirped in delight. "I've already started working on that."

"I know that, my dear Coco." Yashir smiled at me. "You are a tiny bird but you are a brave and intelligent soul. I've lots of hope on you," he said.

I was feeling flattered at the praise of my friend and guide. But the folks before us looked a little confused.

"Heal the collective consciousness?" Johan said in an uncertain note.

"Collective consciousness is all the individual consciousness joined together, right?" Teeber said.

"Right, Teeber," Yashir nodded appreciatively. "We all are part of the collective consciousness."

"Then what do we have to do with healing of the collective consciousness?" Johan looked puzzled. "It sounds too much, you know, for us, the small humans that we are," he said.

"Do you see this little bird, sitting on my shoulder, Johan?" Yashir pointed at me. "Believe me, she has learnt it, and she is already working on that."

A gush of surprise came from the crowd. Everybody was staring at me in awe. I was feeling a little embarrassed. "Please, Yashir," I said, "Tell them that I'm just an ordinary little bird. There is nothing extraordinary about me. It is you who is the leader. I just follow you."

Yashir looked amused at my embarrassment. He ruffled my feathers affectionately. But he went on.

"Look at her. She has lost her kids in the war. She was badly hurt by a war plane and came back from the jaws of death," he said again. "But she forgives those warring humans who killed her kids and was about to rob her of her dear life. She is working on love, on healing the collective consciousness of the planet. If she can do it, you certainly can."

"That's brilliant, Yashir," Jerads said. "She makes us humble. She has set an extraordinary example before us."

"If she can do it, we can do it too," the crowd said in unison.

"Yashir, please tell her that she makes us proud and her example inspires us to transcend our pain and limitations," Johan said, pointing to me.

"She can understand what you say," Yashir said, laughing. "I don't need to translate that for her."

Everybody looked at me with awe in their eyes.

"You're an amazing bird," Johan said to me in applause. "We're inspired to have you with us."

"True little buddy. You are a genius little soul," Adrian joined.

"Thank you," I chirped. "It's very nice of you two to say that." I was shuffling my feet in embarrassment.

Yashir gently smiled at me, and translated for them what I said.

"I wish I could understand your language too," said Sophie, as she walked over to me, to sit near me. She looked secured and happy now. She gently placed her hand on me. I closed my eyes and lifted my face to the moon. This evening has turned so perfect. I didn't want it to end. Everybody was feeling this coziness and the sense of belonging to one another. We were truly feeling like one family.

"I can't wait to begin our new life, Yashir," Teeber said after a while. "In the valley of hope, we'll work to build our paradise. Together we'll work to spread peace and love to every being in the universe."

"Yeah," Adrian echoed Teeber's sentiment. "We'll live in joy, in empathy, understanding and awareness. And together we'll radiate positive and peaceful vibrations to heal the collective consciousness."

"Sure!" Sophie said in dreamy eyes. "We'll work for a peaceful world, a world where no gun will be fired on any living being, where all of our words and thoughts will be harbingers of joy and peace, where even the thoughts of hatred, division and revenge will be alien to humans."

"Now I understand that it is our responsibility to work for a world where our children will be safe, where no life will ever be threatened by guns and bombs," Bella said excitedly.

"Now I can foresee a peaceful earth for my children," Irfana joined. "I can see that our peace and positive vibrations are melting the stony hearts far and near, just as the morning Sun melts the snows on the mountain."

Yashir was all smiles. He said nothing. But he was evidently happy that his folks could finally get the point. Yashir bid them to take rest. Everybody was tired after the long day's walk. Tomorrow morning we'll resume our journey again. The children are fast asleep on the grassy ground.

His folks now looked an inspired lot, driven with a purpose, with a common goal, sharing a noble aspiration. Their eyes shone with a vision, with a noble dream.

I said "Good Night" to Yashir, and flew back to the tree top beside Chico. Today is a full moon day. Moonlight is flooding the distant valley, the mountains and the trees. The earth looks magical under the autumn moon. The gentle breeze of the silent night lulled us in to sleep. Tomorrow our journey will begin again towards a new land and a new future we dream to build up in our valley of hope. We drifted to sleep, cherishing our dreams in our tiny bosoms — the dream of an earth free of the rage of war, crime and sickness; an earth, where all creatures could breathe in peace, respecting one another's right to live in peace and quiet dignity.

ಐ ಐ

ABOUT THE AUTHORS

Dr. Amit Ray is an author, philosopher and spiritual master. He teaches peace, love and compassion for the transformation of human consciousness. He is author of several books on meditation and yoga.

In his early years, he was a scientist. He did his PhD in artificial intelligence and computational neuroscience and worked as a scientist in India, UK and USA. With a spiritual bent of mind from his very childhood, he undertook intense practices in meditation from his early years. In his later years, many mystical experiences prompted him to dedicate his life for the search of truth.

He began sharing his experiences after a series of transformative spiritual awakening. In his Himalayan centre, he lives a life dedicated to meditation, yoga and transformation of human consciousness.

Banani Ray is a mystic, spiritual guide and author of several books on meditation, mysticism and infinite human potential. In her earlier years, while she was teaching in a women's college, she experienced an awakening, and underwent a massive inner transformation.

Her quest for truth motivated her to undertake austere spiritual practices and self-enquiry in solitude. For several years, she lived in Himalaya with her husband Amit, living a life dedicated to meditation and spiritual practices. Over the years, a series of mystic experiences opened up for her the door for profound realization of the underlying interconnectedness and oneness of all beings. She started living her realization, sharing her wisdom and teachings for peace, love and awareness of the unity of consciousness.

Also from Inner Light Publishers

Awakening Inner Guru: The Path of Realizing the God Within

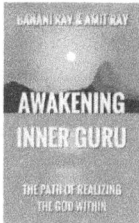

Awakening Inner Guru is a clear and straightforward guide to awaken the light within. For those who are truly interested to attain spiritual freedom and fulfillment in every sphere of life, this book is a practical and personal manual. ISBN: 9788191026900

Laughing Buddha: The Alchemy of Euphoric Living

The spirit of Laughing Buddha is the spirit of ultimate relaxation, happiness and contentment. This book gives a rare combination of ancient Buddhist wisdom and its practical use in our daily lives in the modern world for living in joy. ISBN: 9788191026948

Om Chanting and Meditation

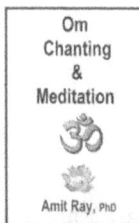

Om is our blissful Self. Om is the mysterious cosmic energy that is the substratum of all the things and all the beings. It is the eternal song of the Divine. This book makes the Om meditation easy to follow, simple to do, and very effective. ISBN: 9788191026931

Yoga and Vipassana: An Integrated Lifestyle

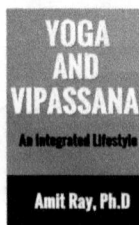

Vipassana Meditation and Yoga are integrated and combined together in this book in a coherent manner. This is intended for those people who want to explore and utilize the benefits of the two ancient techniques of yoga and vipassana in a seamless manner. It is planned for developing deep wisdom, great calmness and joy in life. ISBN: 9788191026924

Affirmations and Visualizations: The Ultimate Secret

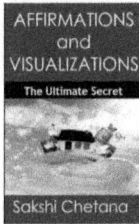

This is a practical and comprehensive guidebook for affirmation and visualization that contains a wealth of practical information, tips, instructions and exercises for improving your life. You will know how and at which level of your mind affirmations and visualization work. You will know the scientific and esoteric secret of working of your mind and how to train your mind to unleash your hidden power. ISBN: 9789382123156

We at Inner Light Publishers are dedicated to publish books that help to improve the quality of human lives. You are welcome to visit us at www.inner-light-in.com